S0-BDZ-488

Ken

Happy Holidays and thank you for your support of Primera Turf

Don't Step
in the
Entremanure!

I hope you will find this little book by one of the Aiteron founders useful in the professional mana-gement of AGRx

Cordially,

Frans

Don't Step in the Entremanure!

Tiptoe Your Way to Entrepreneurial Success

William H. Matthews, Ph.D.

DNLD Publishing

© 2010 DNLD Publishing. Printed and bound in the United States of America. All rights reserved. No part of this book may be reproduced or transmitted in any form or by any means, electronic or mechanical, including photocopying, recording, or by an information storage and retrieval system—except by a reviewer who may quote brief passages in a review to be printed in a magazine, newspaper, or on the Web—without permission in writing from the publisher. For information, please contact DNLD Publishing, 8860 Wildcat Rd., Dayton, OH 45371, 937-669-6510.

Although the author and publisher have made every effort to ensure the accuracy and completeness of information contained in this book, we assume no responsibility for errors, inaccuracies, omissions, or any inconsistency herein. Any slighting of people, places, or organizations is unintentional.

First printing 2010

ISBN 978-1-934282-06-9
LCCN 2008911900

ATTENTION CORPORATIONS, UNIVERSITIES, COLLEGES, AND PRO-FESSIONAL ORGANIZATIONS: Quantity discounts are available on bulk purchases of this book for educational, gift purposes, or as premiums for increasing magazine subscriptions or renewals. Special books or book excerpts can also be created to fit specific needs. For information, please contact DNLD Publishing, 8860 Wildcat Rd., Dayton, OH 45371, 937-669-6510.

ACKNOWLEDGMENTS

TO MY WIFE, Janet, thank you for relentlessly encouraging me to pursue a career that made me happy, even when it meant walking away from other attractive opportunities that have presented themselves along the way. And to my sons, Bob, Todd, Kip, and Trent, I truly appreciate the moral support you have provided, including some very valuable input regarding the format of this book.

I would also like to extend my gratitude to my parents—my mother, Anna, a teacher who instilled in me the desire to write, and my father, Howard, who very successfully grew a privately held company through leadership in action, never asking anyone to do anything he wouldn't do himself.

To Clay Mathile, thank you for inviting me to join you in launching Aileron. Your incredible success at The Iams Company is a real-life example of professional management in action and serves as the basis of the lessons imparted in this book. In fulfilling your own dream through the establishment of Aileron, you have also fulfilled mine.

And to Dave Sullivan, the best "platform" guy I've ever encountered, many thanks for enlightening the owners of privately-held businesses so that they know what a professionally managed organization looks like, laying the groundwork for consultants like me to help with implementation.

To Dan Hackett, Eric Graham, Joni Fedders, and the entire staff of Aileron, thank you for the passion you have for helping privately held businesses implement professional management, create jobs, and improve the quality of life for owners, employees, and the communities where they operate.

And last, but certainly not least, I want to express my appreciation to the hundreds of business owners who have placed their trust in my advice over the years. My hope is that the lessons of this book will help organizational leaders navigate the sometimes rough waters that face them and learn from those who have gone before them, whose stories fill these pages.

CONTENTS

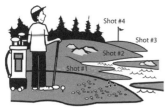

FOREWORD

WINSTON CHURCHILL DEFINED the difference between pessimists and optimists this way: "The optimist sees opportunity in every danger; the pessimist sees danger in every opportunity." Most entrepreneurs I know are straight-up optimists. It takes a certain in-born optimism—that and a set of steady nerves—to take a dream and build it into a business. Or grow an existing enterprise into something bigger and more successful.

In this context, though, optimism can be a two-way street. Yes, it can empower you to accomplish goals that might well surprise you. It can just as easily convince you to ignore the potholes, the red lights, and challenges that crop up along the way. But if you connect with the right people who ask the hard and sometimes uncomfortable questions, they will help you anticipate these challenges. Indeed, you can avoid many of the mistakes I've seen entrepreneurs in every business category make over and over again—and some I made myself. Your journey will be much easier for it.

As a business owner and respected consultant, Bill Matthews has spent a chunk of his life learning about the mistakes that are too often made over and over in the business world. He has asked the right questions and challenged business leaders to think through their actions. In this book, Bill offers an in-depth look at the common and not-so-common mistakes business owners make, and he asks questions that will help you steer your ship clear of the rocks.

Many of these lessons I learned the hard way. After taking over The Iams Company in 1982, I quickly realized I had to make basic changes in my approach to running the business. It was only by surrounding myself with experienced people who asked challenging questions—the ones that made me take a good hard look at myself and my business—that I was able to grow Iams.

Save yourself some trouble. Learn how to sidestep what Bill calls the "entremanure" with this book. It's about more than just avoiding mistakes—it's about capitalizing on opportunities while being aware of the implications of the real world today, tomorrow, and all the tomorrows to come.

Pay special attention to the questions at the end of each chapter. They'll help you think more deeply about yourself and your business. If you find you fall short in some areas, take heart! It means you've identified a potential problem, which in turn means you can figure a way to step around it.

It also means that, like Winston Churchill's optimist, you will have identified an opportunity.

Clay Mathile

CHAPTER 1

Learn from the Successes and Failures of Others

THE STATISTICS REGARDING business failures are intimidating. The failure rate could be significantly reduced, however, if business owners would simply learn from the successes and failures of others!

Although this book provides information that should be of help to those who already have a business, as well as those who are about to start one, *the primary focus will be on those who have already negotiated their way through the start-up phase.* That is, it's based on the successes and failures of those who have gone before you.

After working with hundreds of established, privately-held businesses, I've found there are a number of common areas where business owners struggle. Therefore, the chapters that follow provide some insight about the challenges that are most often encountered. They're the steps entrepreneurs sometimes take that they would like the chance to do over again—steps that have led them into muck and mire, which I like to call "entremanure!"

In trying to determine the most effective way to present these potential pitfalls, I decided to rely on four factors I have observed in most entrepreneurs. First, brevity is king; the less time they have to spend reading, the better. Second, they like to see each principle clearly stated, almost like the Ten Commandments (hence, the title of each chapter is presented that way). Third, they always seem to want examples of what to do or not to do. Fourth, they rely heavily on checklists or questions that enable them to determine whether or not they're on the right track.

Therefore, this is precisely the format in which this book is presented—it's brief, and each chapter title is stated as a principle. An example follows each explanation, and a checklist is presented at the end of each chapter so readers can see whether they've stepped in the "entremanure!"

Before you go on to the next chapter, you might find if insightful to go through the list of questions below to determine the general health of your business. There are thirty-two questions. The objective is to answer "yes" to all thirty-two, but it's unlikely that even the healthiest companies will be able to score that high. At the very least, your answers should help you focus on the areas where your business needs the most improvement.

At the end of the list you will find instructions on how to interpret your score and where to focus your efforts.

Category I: Leadership (7 Questions)

1. Do you have a long-term vision for your organization, and is it clearly articulated to all employees?
2. Are *you* capable of leading the organization to achieve the vision you have established?
3. Is your current management team capable of taking the organization where you want it to go?
4. Do you have an *independent* outside board that does *not* include shareholders, friends, family, your accountant, attorney, banker, or others whose advice you are already paying to get?
5. Do you have an updated organizational chart?
6. Do you have a succession plan to cover key positions in your organization?
7. Do you find you are able to retain your strong employees?

Category II: Finance, Administration, Planning, and Control (7 Questions)

8. Do you have a strategic plan that is regularly updated and covers at least a three-year period?

9. Do you have annual budgets, and do you monitor performance against them?

10. Do your financial reports accurately reflect profitability details for each product, service, department, and customer group?

11. Do you have—and use—an up-to-date employee handbook?

12. Do you have updated job descriptions for everyone in your organization, including yourself?

13. Do you conduct formal performance appraisals with every employee at least once each year?

14. Do you have established, well-documented pay ranges and rankings for each position?

Category III: Marketing and Sales (10 Questions)

15. Is the technology of your product or service at least on par with that of your strongest competitor?

16. Have you clearly defined who your target customers are and who they are not?

17. Do you know your current market-share percentage?

18. Are you gaining market share?

19. Do you know who your competitors are and who they will be in the future?

20. Do you know the strengths and weaknesses of each major competitor and how they compare to you?

21. Is your quality at least as good as the quality of your strongest competitor?

22. Is at least 30 percent of your "typical" sales person's compensation based on performance incentives?

23. Are your sales representatives successfully bringing in new business that will fuel your long-term growth?

24. Do your sales representatives have specific target accounts and submit regular call reports?

25. Do you have a clear focus as to whether you are a low-priced/low-cost competitor or a highly-differentiated/higher-cost marketer?

Category IV: Productivity and Accountability of Employees (8 Questions)

26. Are your sales per employee at least equal to the average for your industry?

27. Are people truly being held accountable in your organization (including corrective actions and rewards)?

28. Are you willing to replace people when necessary, even if they happen to be related to you?

29. Are you bringing in stronger employees to replace those who leave?

30. Does each employee have specific, quantitative standards by which performance is measured regularly?

31. Does each employee's compensation have a component that provides an incentive when performance standards are exceeded?

32. Are year-end bonuses based on specific, quantitative goals, rather than on the discretion of the owner or leader?

How Well Did You Score?

If you honestly answered "yes" to all thirty-two questions, you're in a very elite group! In general, a score of twenty-six or higher is good. The goal is to *score high in all four categories*— that is, if you answered "no" to more than two questions in any category, it would be wise to focus your efforts in those areas that need attention. Regardless of your score, I hope the pages that follow will provide you with insight on how to avoid future pitfalls so that you *don't step in the entremanure!"*

CHAPTER 2

Build a Business with the Intent That the Enterprise Will Continue, Even If You Plan to Sell It Some Day

THE RAPID GROWTH of the Internet, and technology in general, has fostered new businesses that have significantly altered "the way we've always done it." In many cases, the entrepreneurs who have so creatively crafted these new enterprises have done so with the intention of quickly selling them or taking them public.

Although it certainly makes sense for every business and entrepreneur to have an exit strategy, it's important to build a business that can be sustained over the long term in the event that the exit strategy doesn't materialize. Many of the early "dot-com" businesses learned this lesson the hard way. It's like building a house—the foundation must first be constructed properly.

Building a business with the intention of operating it for a long time can be especially important if the enterprise is seeking outside investors. It was probably best said by a wealthy investor who made the following comment after reviewing a number of business plans in the late 1990s: "I'm really tired of having people ask me to invest in their companies when it seems like all they want to do is 'cash in' as soon as they can. Doesn't anybody ever want to build an enterprise and stick with it? A business built on solid ground with a sustained record of growth in sales and earnings will typically have a lot of alternative methods of 'exit' available to it."

There are a number of ways that ownership of a business can be transferred—selling to an outsider, selling to employees, transitioning ownership to family members, or "going public," among others. The fact is, it doesn't matter how you plan to "exit"; any prospective owner will want some assurance that the business is going to continue. That means the organization should have a good product or service, in a solid market, with a highly qualified management team. Many transactions fall apart because a prospective buyer is disappointed in the management team, even though the product and market offer substantial growth potential.

Even more importantly, consider what might happen if the owner of a business suddenly passes away or becomes permanently disabled. If the business isn't built on a solid foundation, including capable employees, failure can occur very quickly, eroding the equity and jeopardizing the estate that is left behind. Many businesses have life insurance policies covering the owner, with the company as beneficiary, as a means of protecting the company in the event of the owner's unexpected death. Although this is certainly a good idea, it's no substitute for having strong managers in place who can step in to bring the organization through the transition. Indeed, if the company has truly been established with the intent to continue, all safeguards will be in place.

Example

Charles was a bright, aggressive young polymer chemist who worked for a large manufacturer of building products. At age twenty-five, he cashed in his 401K and raised some investment money from relatives and friends to launch a new company to manufacture plastic wood for exterior use. He had developed a method of producing this product using scrap materials and convinced investors he would quickly generate tremendous volume due to the high demand for the product, particularly in residential decks. His plan was to make an initial public offering within five years, thereby providing an attractive exit strategy for all investors, including himself.

By the end of the third year Charles was making good progress in the marketplace, although still below his projections. He was in the process of seeking more investors to help him accelerate his presence in the market when, as if from out of nowhere, a large manufacturer and distributor of building products launched a huge marketing effort to introduce a similar product that was physically more attractive (looked more like real wood), stronger, lighter, and less expensive. In addition, because of its established network of distributors in the industry, the new product was immediately available to the public. The business that Charles had established quickly slipped into major financial difficulties, culminating in liquidation.

If Charles had originally planned to build a sustainable business rather than aimed at an initial public offering, he may have taken a different approach by partnering with a company that already had strong distribution established in the industry. Investment dollars could have been earmarked for product improvements and cost reductions, rather than establishing distribution. Building a business for the long term requires a lot of thought as to what the future will bring and how the company will be prepared to deal with changes in the market and competition; get-rich-quick strategies are rarely successful.

Check Your Shoes...

Before you move on to the next chapter, check the bottoms of your shoes to see whether you've avoided the entremanure:

- Did you set out with the intention that your business will be around for a long time?

- What do you see yourself, personally, doing in five years?

- Do you have a long-term vision for the company? Can you explain it to others? Are you excited about it?

- Have you surrounded yourself with people who are excited about your vision?

- Do employees see a long-term commitment from you and good career paths for themselves?

- Imagine for a moment that you don't own or work at your company but are interviewing for a position there—would you want to become an employee?

.

CHAPTER 3

Be Sure You Have Enough Money to Sustain What You Have Started

THERE ARE SOME alarming statistics regarding the number and percentage of business failures each year. Sometimes those statistics are a little misleading. For example, there are many individuals who start a business, fail, start another business, fail again, and then finally succeed after their third attempt. This is recorded as two failures and one success, even though all three attempts were by the same individual rather than three separate people. It's often the same business, restarted by the same person, that succeeds the second or third time, after failing earlier.

A friend of mine told me he once attended a seminar where a guest in the room had been tremendously successful with three different companies during his career. After a number of attendees had complimented him on his achievements, he finally admitted, "Everyone is always giving me credit for those three companies. What most people don't know is that I actually had nine different companies, but the other six were failures."

One major reason for business failure is under-capitalization—that is, the enterprise just doesn't have enough money to get it through the early stages of development. Time and time again, there are hard-working, intelligent entrepreneurs who have a great business plan, are making good progress, but have to close their doors because they run out of money. To add insult to injury, often someone else comes along with the same business plan, sometimes in the same location, and operates successfully by carrying out what the first business owner could have done if the money had not run out. Some people call it "timing," but it's really a matter of being able to weather the financial storm until the business can sustain itself.

Although there are no hard and fast rules regarding the amount of money you need before launching a business, a general guideline is to make sure you have enough money to survive for at least three years without taking any dollars out of the business. Depending on the type of business and economic or market conditions, you should plan on as long as five years. If the business isn't breaking even or making a profit after year three, there may be reason to doubt whether the enterprise will ever be profitable. On the other hand, if the business is generating a profit at the end of year three (or sooner), it's likely that a bank will be ready to step in and help with a line of credit.

Estimating the amount of money needed to sustain a business through the initial years is not an easy task. In fact, even those who consider themselves astute business people often rely on outside help to prepare realistic projections of business performance so that they get an independent, professional perspective.

A huge challenge is cash flow. Many companies that are making profits on paper are unable to pay their bills (or worse yet, their employees) because they are cash poor. Items like inventory and receivables can tie up a lot of cash and make it difficult to meet day-to-day obligations. A good accountant or financial advisor can help project monthly cash flow based on expected sales and expenses.

Example

Mama was very proud of her Italian heritage. She and her husband, Joseph, raised their three children in an active household that was often filled with neighborhood friends and schoolmates, who always raved about Mama's pizza.

After the children were on their own, Mama and Joseph decided to take the advice of so many people who had urged them to open a pizza store. They took a second mortgage on their house, found a great location in the neighborhood, bought the necessary equipment, and opened Mama's Italian Pizza Shop.

Many of the people in the neighborhood were frequent patrons, but sales grew only gradually. Fourteen months later Mama and Joseph could no longer sustain the business, even though they had reached break-even that month. The losses from the previous thirteen months had reached a point where they were unable to meet their financial obligations.

Three months after the closing of Mama's Italian Pizza Shop, a new pizza shop opened in the same building. It was operated by a former business executive, of Italian heritage, who loved to cook and had received a nice severance package from his previous employer. He had plenty of money and, according to the local newspaper, "was looking for something fun to do." As with Mama, things started out a little slowly for him, but he was able to meet his financial obligations and also had the necessary funds to spend on promotion in the community. The business thrived and, ironically, he hired Mama as manager—not what she had hoped for originally, but she eventually became a minority shareholder...if only she had had enough money at the outset.

Check Your Shoes…

Before you move on to the next chapter, check the bottoms of your shoes to see whether you've avoided the entremanure:

- Have you taken the time to lay out (realistically) how much money you'll need to survive for three to five years?

- Have you had an *independent, objective* outside business advisor help you evaluate your financial expectations? Sales? Expenses? Timing?

- Do you have alternative financial resources to "tap" if you fall short?

- Do you have a *thorough* understanding of the difference between profit and cash flow? If someone asked you to explain how a company can be profitable but not have sufficient cash to continue operating, could you do it?

CHAPTER 4

Hire the Best People Available

THIS IS, BY FAR, *the most important advice in this book!* Today's entrepreneurs are burdened by many employees who are not capable of moving the company forward. Unfortunately, these are often employees who have been with the entrepreneur for a long time, maybe even from the very beginning. They are often family members! *No matter who they are, if they are not capable of moving you forward, you must make a change!*

If you had a machine that was not performing, you'd replace it with a better one as soon as you could. Why, then, would anyone allow a substandard performer to continue performing a function that he or she is no longer capable of performing effectively? The answer is not a simple one. Nor is it easy to make a change when you may have a close personal relationship (or are related to) the employee in question. But consider the effect that this situation might be having on others in your organization who resent it and whose performance might be slipping because of it. It's the old "why should I work hard when Charlie is retired on the job" syndrome, and it can be devastating to morale and productivity.

It doesn't mean that the substandard performer needs to be terminated. In fact, remember that *you* are probably the one who promoted him or her to the current position, so you are partly to blame for the situation. The right thing to do is first look for another position in the organization where this person will be productive, which is likely to be *at least* one level below his or her current level. Of course, this often means a reduction in salary, but keep in mind that you must be fair to others in the organization. The results of making a change like this might surprise you. I recently met with a client who finally demoted his vice president of manufacturing to a lower-level position, and the employee was elated because he knew he wasn't capable of doing the job and felt like he was "letting the company down." Will everyone react in that way? Absolutely not, but what's right is right.

How do you tell someone they're being demoted or terminated after a long career? The answer is simple—make the employee part of the solution. Meet with the employee and discuss his or her performance. Establish quantifiable objectives (standards of performance) that you expect the employee to meet, and then *ask the employee what help he or she needs from you in order to meet those objectives.* It's important that you both agree on the objectives, that you establish a reasonable timeframe within which those objectives are to be met, and agree on progressively more severe consequences if those objectives are not attained. *Do this while sitting on the same side of the desk, so that the employee knows you truly want him or her to succeed and that you'll provide whatever help is necessary.* Surprisingly, many employees respond by meeting the goals, but most often this is only a temporary phenomenon. In the end, the vast majority fall short, are demoted or terminated, or leave very soon after you first meet with them. The bottom line is that *you have been fair.*

Of course, the best advice is to avoid over-promoting people. Always ask yourself what type of person you'll need in a job when your business grows by 50 to 100 percent. Then, select the very best candidate available, whether from inside or outside the company. Is this going to be more expensive? You bet, but you can't afford *not* to do it!

How do you know whether an employee has been over-promoted? You can usually tell by the way the person accepts responsibility, authority, and accountability. If you find you have to keep going back to an employee to make sure something is getting done correctly, or if the employee keeps delegating responsibility *back* to you, then there's a problem. You hear a lot today about "empowering your employees," but you can't empower them if they're not capable of accepting the empowerment.

"If I go outside, how do I know I've found a good employee?" The answer to this question will be covered in the next chapter, but in general, be very careful when you find someone who seems to be a bargain. For example, a company's leaders were recently looking for someone who could develop new business. They located a salesman in his late forties who was willing to work for $50,000 per year. After they hired him, they realized why he was available for just $50,000 per year. There are sometimes bargain hires in the employment market, but they're rare, and they tend to be those who are in the early stages of their careers, just waiting to blossom in the right environment.

Many companies today utilize pre-employment testing to assess whether a candidate is suited for a particular position in the company. Done properly, assessment testing can be a great screening device that will help you avoid making the wrong selection and also keep the candidate from entering a position he or she might regret later. These tests can also be used with existing employees you may be considering for advancement. A professional assessment can be performed that measures the employee's competence in the specific areas most critical to success as outlined in the job description. I've often seen occasions when a top sales performer was promoted to sales manager but performed very poorly in the new role due to a lack of management skill. Top sales people often find it difficult to manage and develop the skills of others; they'd rather sell!

Also keep in mind that assessment tests are often effective tools when hiring employees for the factory floor. In addition to the obvious advantage of determining how a candidate's personality will "fit" with the established culture, there are some other creative ways testing can be utilized. For example, consider the company that was having difficulty hiring welders who would perform well and would "fit" within the organization. The owner asked a few of the company's top-performing, best-liked welders to be studied by a professional assessment company. Those who conducted the assessments isolated common characteristics among the welders they studied and designed a specific assessment test that enabled the company to identify potential welders most likely to be good performers and well-liked. The company began to utilize the new test when interviewing candidates and soon found it had significantly reduced turnover and increased productivity.

Example

Marilyn and Joanne worked together at a telemarketing company for seven years. The two ladies became very close friends and were also extremely successful telemarketers.

When Marilyn received an inheritance, she decided to start a telemarketing company of her own. She knew Joanne was one of the most productive and aggressive telemarketers she had ever worked with, so she invited Joanne to join her at the new company.

Initially, the two worked side-by-side on the phones, even though Marilyn was the owner and occasionally had to call on clients and develop additional business. As the company grew, additional telemarketers were hired, and it became necessary to appoint a manager of the group. For Marilyn, the obvious choice was Joanne; after all, Joanne had the most experience, was Marilyn's closest friend, and had been with the new company from the very first day. Soon, there were nine telemarketers reporting to Joanne, but employee turnover was steadily increasing. Marilyn knew that turnover was an industry-wide problem due to the nature of the work, but the rate had reached a level that was nearly double the industry average.

To study the situation more closely, Marilyn began to conduct exit interviews. It soon became apparent that the aggressive personality that made Joanne such a successful telemarketer was the very reason so many people were leaving. She confronted Joanne, and Joanne agreed to attend a seminar to develop her management and interpersonal skills. When the turnover rate continued to run high and exit interviews still indicated Joanne was the major cause, Marilyn asked Joanne if she would be willing participate in an assessment test. Joanne agreed, but the results were not what she had hoped to see. The assessment indicated Joanne's aggressiveness was so strong and deeply-rooted that it was highly unlikely she could ever be successful in a role where she managed people.

After many candid, heart-to-heart discussions, Marilyn and Joanne came to an agreement. Joanne would remain with the company, would continue to report directly to Marilyn, and would be responsible for business-to-business telemarketing calls. She would take a reduction in base pay because no one would be reporting to her, but she would be given an incentive compensation plan that would reward her for her productivity. A new supervisor was hired to replace Joanne. The employee turnover rate improved significantly after the change was made. Although it was a difficult decision for Marilyn, she had convinced Joanne that the company had done everything in its power to deal with the problem in a way that was fair to everyone. Joanne is still with the company, but today she also serves as the trainer for new employees before they begin their work as telemarketers.

Check Your Shoes...

Before you move on to the next chapter, check the bottoms of your shoes to see whether you've avoided the entremanure:

- If your company doubled in size, do you have the management people in place to handle the change? More importantly, would *you* still be capable of leading the company?

- If you were away from the business for an extended period of time, could it operate without you? Do you find that people are delegating their duties back to you?

- Do you have any employees or partners who are so good on the job you fear someone will hire them away from you? What are you doing to prevent it?

- Do you have quantitative standards of performance for all employees?

- Do you have financial incentives for employees? If so, are the incentives tied to the performance measures relevant to what they do?

- Are there people in your organization who are substandard performers? If so, are you trying to help them overcome their shortcomings? If you've tried unsuccessfully to help them improve, do you have a compassionate yet firm plan to help them find employment elsewhere in a position suited for them?

CHAPTER 5

To Avoid Future Personnel Problems, Hire the Right People at the Outset

TERMINATING EMPLOYEES IS not fun. Although it may sound obvious, you can significantly reduce the number of terminations by hiring the right people at the outset.

Determining whom to hire is very challenging for most of us. The ideal candidate for the job must have more than just technical skills; "chemistry" is vitally important. No matter how many screening techniques you use, there is no guarantee that you'll hire the right person.

In many cases you're better off hiring someone you have worked with before (*but not someone who is a close friend or relative*), even if that person is not a perfect fit for the position. Work ethic, personal value system, and attitude on the job are essential ingredients that are difficult to detect during an interview, but if you've already had the opportunity to work with someone on a regular basis, you're in a much better position to predict how they will perform. Interviewing is a skill that can and should be learned through professional training. Taking the time to learn how to interview can pay enormous dividends by reducing the risk of making a poor hiring decision that has to be reversed later.

As stated in the previous chapter, many companies rely on personality tests in making hiring decisions. A personality test that is properly administered and interpreted can provide very valuable information regarding a candidate, particularly if those who administer the test can compare the results with a profile of the duties the candidate would be performing on the job. Effective testing can be an excellent source of information regarding the future behavior that can be expected from a candidate in a particular position. It's normally relatively inexpensive to have a candidate professionally tested, especially if the test uncovers information that will help you avoid the future expense and trauma associated with making a bad hiring decision requiring termination.

Another technique that improves the probability you'll make a good hiring decision is to adopt the "temp-to-hire" strategy, whereby you first bring someone in on a temporary basis so you can evaluate the candidate on the job before making a hiring decision. Although it can be a bit expensive to pay the going rate for temporary employees supplied by an outside company, it usually reduces the likelihood that a poor hiring decision will be made.

It's certainly important to check the references supplied by an applicant. In addition, it's a good idea to do some further investigating on your own. For example, if you see that the applicant has worked at XYZ Company, and you happen to know someone who works there, it may be worthwhile for you to find out what it's like to work with the applicant. Some companies make a practice of calling the applicant at home, unannounced, to find out whether the applicant has any questions about the job and just to see how the applicant says "hello" when answering the phone. It's important to remember that under no circumstances should you carry your investigation beyond the limits of good judgment, ethics, or personal privacy.

As a general rule, if an applicant has been laid off or is the victim of a "reduction in force" at his or her last place of employment, it could be at least a "yellow flag" (and possibly a "red flag"). In my working life, I don't ever recall laying off an employee I thought was a star performer—and star performers are the only candidates you should be hiring. Of course, there are exceptions. There are also situations where an entire company shuts down or moves out of town—indeed, in cases like that there are likely to be many star performers left without work. My only point is that you should be cautious about hiring anyone whose previous employer let the person get away for any reason.

Example

The owner of a financial services company had grown his organization to about seventy-five employees when his outside board recommended that he become chairman and bring in an experienced president who could take the company to the next level.

After a lot of discussion and deliberation, he agreed to search for an outsider who could move the company forward. He interviewed a number of people from the industry and, with the help of his board, selected a candidate who had nearly twenty years of experience, including a position as president at a competing company in another region of the country.

Although the candidate brought the necessary expertise, it quickly became apparent that his personality and leadership style were significantly different from what had been developed by the owner during the prior twenty years. Before the end of the first year, the owner terminated the new president and began to run the business by himself, just as he had done in the past.

With the owner back at the helm, his outside board soon saw the same pattern of management and direction that had earlier compelled the recommendation of a new president. The board urged the owner to renew his search, advising him that it was still the right thing to do, even though he chose the wrong candidate the first time. As an interim measure, the owner agreed to bring in a consultant to help with some of the specific issues stifling the company's growth. One of the board members recommended a consultant whom he thought could help. The owner interviewed the consultant, liked what he saw, and invited the consultant to assist him over a period of six months.

By the fifth month, the employees of the company had repeatedly told the owner how great the consultant was. He was providing the help they needed and culturally was a great "fit." When the owner reported these things to the board, its members suggested he approach the consultant to see whether he would consider becoming president. After all, aside from the fact that the consultant had limited experience in that particular industry, he had demonstrated his ability to lead in a manner that was highly acceptable to both the owner and the employees.

The owner made an attractive offer, and the consultant accepted. Combining the vision of the owner with the management skills of the new president, the organization experienced unprecedented growth during the next four years, culminating in the sale of the company to a national competitor.

Check Your Shoes…

Before you move on to the next chapter, check the bottoms of your shoes to see whether you've avoided the entremanure:

- Do you have a good track record for identifying and hiring strong performers? If not, what steps are you taking to improve?
- Would a potential employee be excited to enter the working environment at your company?
- Do you have detailed job descriptions, and do you hire employees who possess the important characteristics in your job descriptions?
- Do you hire people who are currently working rather than those who are not?

- Do you identify people you would like to recruit, even though they're not looking for another position, and then seek them out as possible employees?

- Do you check references, including a little extra investigation to locate possible references that might not have been provided by the applicant?

- Do you use personality tests to identify potential "fits" with your company culture?

CHAPTER 6

Don't Promote Employees to Management Positions without Proper Training

IF YOU THINK back to your first real job as an adult, you were probably hired because of some technical ability for which you had been formally trained. Perhaps you started as an accountant, computer programmer, or toolmaker. In those early years of your career, you spent the vast majority of your time doing what you had been trained to do.

As you gained experience, you probably began to assume some management or supervisory responsibilities. By this time, your workday may have been split evenly between doing what you were trained to do and watching over others who were placed under your wing.

Then one day you looked around and found your day was predominantly consumed by managing others rather than doing what you had been formally trained to do. Yet you probably had little or no formal training as a manager—is it any wonder why many managers feel a little overwhelmed? Worse yet, we often continue to promote people until they fail—then we terminate them when, in fact, their failure may have been due to our own unwillingness to train them.

Management training is extremely important. Even after some people have been thoroughly trained to function as professional managers, many are not effective or prefer to revert back to the activity that first interested them—such as accounting, computer programming, or toolmaking.

Just as it's essential to remove poor performers from your management team, so it's also essential that you, as the leader of the enterprise, be willing to remove yourself from the top spot if you realize you are no longer effective in that role. Many owners find life is much more fun for them and that the business operates much more smoothly when they bring in a professional manager to run things and devote their own efforts to what they like most.

Example

As a young girl growing up in Iowa, Kate became very interested in tropical fish. It was a hobby that consumed her spare time, until she decided to open a tropical fish distribution operation at age twenty-five.

Kate was truly an expert in tropical fish. She had developed contacts all over the world who could supply the fish she needed at prices that would allow her to make attractive gross margins when selling them to retail pet stores. Her other strong competency was in medicating fish so that they were delivered alive and healthy to her customers, a major advantage she had achieved over her competitors.

The company grew to more than one million dollars in sales, and Kate continued to add employees to fill orders for shipment, which involved selecting the correct fish from hundreds of tanks in her warehouse and packing them properly to ensure they would be healthy when customers received them.

As she added more and more employees, the job soon became too much for her. The two duties that Kate could not delegate to anyone else were medicating the fish and ordering them from her established worldwide network. She sought the advice of a local business acquaintance to find out how she could distribute her workload.

Her advisor helped her realize she needed to focus on medicating and ordering the fish. Eventually, Kate admitted she wasn't the most experienced person when it came to things like warehouse layout, order picking, shipping, or selecting and scheduling employees in the warehouse. Her first inclination was to run an ad in the newspaper seeking someone who could supervise warehouse people, with a modest but competitive compensation package. Her advisor convinced her, however, that she needed a higher-level employee who could fill all of the gaps in her warehouse operation.

Together, Kate and her advisor decided to search for someone in an industry with similar characteristics—perishable products that need to be delivered overnight. They agreed to find a candidate from the fresh produce industry who could help them organize the warehouse, develop a system for tracking inventory, picking and packing orders, and introducing barcode technology to the warehouse.

Today, Kate is still president, but the company's activities are split into two major categories. Kate oversees purchasing and medicating fish, and all other internal operations are handled by Taylor, Director of Operations, who joined her from the produce industry. Taylor saw a great career opportunity with Kate's growing company, and Kate made the decision to bring Taylor in at a salary level commensurate with the position. The operation runs far more smoothly than before, and it's likely Taylor will be able to handle the job even after the company triples in size. At the same time, Kate is gradually training Taylor in the medication and purchase of fish so that someday, perhaps, Taylor can replace Kate and a new Director of Operations can be hired to fill the vacancy created by Taylor's promotion.

Although it was certainly a financial strain for Kate to hire and train a person the caliber of Taylor, Kate did not view it as an expense, but as an *investment* in the future, which would provide a return.

Check Your Shoes...

Before you move on to the next chapter, check the bottoms of your shoes to see whether you've avoided the entremanure:

- Do you like to manage people? If not, what do you *really* like to do?

- Are you *good* at managing people? Do your employees think you're good at it?

- Are you capable of—and looking forward to—managing the people in your organization as you get more and more employees?

- Is there anyone else in your organization who has strong management skills?

CHAPTER 7

Communicate with Your Employees on a Regular Basis

EMPLOYEES ALWAYS SEEM to complain about the lack of communication in an organization. They feel like they're in the dark and not aware of the vision and direction that has been established by the leader of the business. They're "left out."

Actually, poor communication in an organization is usually just a *symptom* of some other underlying weakness. Typically, the companies whose employees complain about lack of communication can blame the structure of the organization itself and/or the managers and supervisors whose job it is to "carry the message" up, down, and across the organization.

It starts at the top. A strong leader surrounds himself or herself with a strong cadre of managers, keeps them continuously informed, and asks for their input. These managers, in turn, do the same with the employees who report to them. If you're convinced that your management team is strong, and employees still feel like they're in the dark, then look at the structure of the organization itself; it's likely you'll find the cause there. Are job descriptions in place and up to date? Are lines of authority and responsibility clearly established? Are there specific, measurable performance standards? Are employees held accountable to meet those standards?

Sometimes there are simply too many employees reporting to one manager, which can make it very difficult for the manager to communicate regularly with employees, no matter how hard the manager tries.

One very successful business owner attributed much of her company's phenomenal growth to the fact that the vision of the enterprise was so well communicated to every level of the organization that even the custodian could explain it without hesitation. As a result, the company has also received incredible input from employees at all levels who have discovered better ways to do things—they're now part of the solution!

My experience has been that business owners who have clearly and consistently articulated their vision for the company have had very few complaints about lack of communication. That is, employees know the vision that has been established for the company, and they understand their specific roles in achieving that vision. Simply stated, there is a common focus. If your employees are complaining about poor communications, I'd suggest you first examine your own vision for your organization to see whether you, yourself, can articulate where you want to take the company. Assuming your vision is clear, then ask some of your employees what *they* think the vision is for the company. In most cases, you'll quickly discover a disconnect. If you can clarify the vision to everyone on a consistent and continuous basis, it's likely that there will be very few complaints about communication.

How do most leaders solve the problem of poor communications when employees complain? They launch an employee newsletter. Although employee newsletters are certainly worthwhile, they are no substitute for the day-to-day, real time communication that is so essential to growth and healthy morale throughout an organization.

Finally, never underestimate the impact your actions will have on communications. Verbally communicating one thing to employees while non-verbally sending another message leaves employees with mixed signals. When that happens, the tendency is for employees to ignore the verbal message but take note of the non-verbal one.

Example

After a successful career with a large corporation in the tele-communications industry, Randy took early retirement to start his own company as a supplier to that same industry.

Randy had a very dynamic, charismatic personality and a great vision for the company. His own employees referred to him as "a visionary." They rallied around him, and the company grew to eighty employees within two years. The activity level each day was fun and fast-paced. The office was laid out in a wide-open environment so that communication was enhanced. By design, there were only a few offices with doors, plus a private conference room. Employees were energized, focused on Randy's vision, and felt like they were always "informed," even though the fast pace made it difficult for Randy to set aside any special time to communicate verbally with employees.

One Friday morning when Randy had called together his six top mangers for a meeting, he raised the topic of expense control. He was particularly concerned about air travel expense and reminded the managers that they were to take greater care in purchasing the very lowest possible airfares. After a fifteen-minute discussion, the meeting moved to another topic, at which point there was a knock at the door. Randy's administrative assistant, Carol, excused herself for interrupting, stood in the doorway, and said to Randy for all to hear: "Randy, the only first-class seat available for your flight to Atlanta is Delta's early morning departure on Monday. The price is $1,200. I can get you a less expensive seat on another flight later that morning, but I know you won't fly anything but first class, so I booked it."

The office chatter after the meeting reached epic proportions. The open-office environment that had been so good for communications had worked to Randy's disadvantage. By noon, everyone had heard the story. Randy never totally recovered the respect it had taken him so long to build among his employees. Things weren't quite the same after that, and soon there were complaints that the employees weren't receiving enough communication from the top.

Check Your Shoes...

Before you move on to the next chapter, check the bottoms of your shoes to see whether you've avoided the entremanure:

- How well do know your employees? How well do they know you?

- Is your vision for the company clearly stated and understood? If your employees were asked what your vision is for the company, would they be able to explain it accurately?

- Does each employee know how his or her job fits into the overall plan for the company?

- Do you ask for and value the opinions of employees and partners?

- Do you respond to questions and suggestions from employees, even if they seem unimportant to you?

CHAPTER 8

Have a Succession Plan

IF YOU'VE FOLLOWED some of the other advice mentioned in the earlier chapters, then you probably have at least one strong candidate who is groomed to step in if something should happen to you.

Unfortunately, most entrepreneurs prefer to have as much control as possible and are therefore likely to have surrounded themselves with people who are not used to—or not able to— make decisions. Here again, having a strong management team in place will help sustain the business in your absence.

If you don't feel like you can take a vacation for a few days, then you probably don't have a potential successor in place. If you're fortunate enough to have a strong successor in your organization, make sure you take good care of that employee! Be sure you have formally communicated your choice to your spouse or another key advisor so that your wishes can be met in the event you cannot communicate the choice yourself.

Succession planning goes beyond your own replacement. If you have an organization filled with managers who are middle-aged and older, with no young "water-walkers" coming up through the ranks, then it could be because you've cut off the supply of new, younger talent so crucial to your continued success. If the strong young people in your organization are leaving, take a good look at the organization to make sure you haven't created an obstruction.

If your company is filled with people who are extremely talented in a particular technical field, take a close look to see whether anyone has a business background to help with the aspects of day-to-day activities not covered by the multitude of technologists. Also, seek the help of an outside board that can help guide you on the business issues. I've often seen companies that honestly "don't know what they don't know" when it comes to the business side of things. A board can help you identify potential successors, not only for yourself but also for other key people in your organization.

Even if you do have a succession plan, it's often a good idea to have "key man insurance" on yourself, with the company as the beneficiary. In the event of your unexpected death, the company will receive the funds from your life insurance policy, which can be utilized to buy back the stock from your estate.

Example

When Jim graduated from high school in 1965, he joined his father's tool and die business as a toolmaker. In 1987 Jim's father implemented a plan to turn the business gradually over to Jim, who was now forty years old. By 1992 Jim was sole owner of the company and began to implement a number of changes.

A key challenge for Jim was the aging workforce. The number of toolmakers in the marketplace was limited. A very popular profession when Jim left high school had lost favor over the years, and Jim knew the shortage of workers would be a major deterrent to growth in the future.

Jim's company was still small when he officially took over as owner, with just twenty employees. Yet the demand, primarily from the automotive industry, continued to be strong. Sales volume did not present a problem for him since the customer base and relationships were very strong. Therefore, Jim focused on recruiting and training new employees who could help the company grow. The remainder of his "non-production" staff was very small since margins had become extremely tight in the industry. Nonetheless, Jim's company continued to make progress due primarily to his own personal ability to recruit and train new employees.

On the night before Thanksgiving, 1996, Jim complained of pain in his left arm. He knew it was symptomatic of a heart problem, so his wife took him to the emergency room. Two days later he underwent quadruple bypass surgery.

His surgery had been successful, but three days later Jim developed a blood clot that traveled through his heart while he slept. Jim never woke up. He had died unexpectedly before his fiftieth birthday.

Jim had no outside board and had not communicated to anyone what his plans were for succession. To complicate matters further, no one from his limited administrative staff was capable of stepping in to take over, not even on a temporary basis. The only person who might possibly have been able to help out was his father, but in 1995 he had been diagnosed with Alzheimer's disease. Sadly, there was no "key man" insurance policy on Jim's life, so the company did not have the funds to buy Jim's stock from his estate.

Left with no other viable alternative, the family sold the business to a competitor for $700,000. Ironically, this same competitor had approached Jim eleven months earlier about buying the business for $950,000, with the assumption that Jim would stay with the company for at least six months after the transaction. Without Jim to show the competitor how to recruit and train new employees and to help with the existing customers, the business was not worth as much.

The new owners moved the business to a location about seven miles away, retaining all the toolmakers and most of the customers. Unfortunately, two of Jim's administrative people were left without jobs after the move.

Check Your Shoes...

Before you move on to the next chapter, check the bottoms of your shoes to see whether you've avoided the entremanure:

- Do you have a will? Is it up to date?

- Is there someone who could take over your company if you died or became incapacitated in some way?

- Do you have life insurance, with the company as the primary beneficiary, so that the company could purchase your stock from your spouse or estate?

- Is there a person already identified, inside or outside the company, who could step in temporarily to manage the company in your unexpected absence?

- Are your wishes in writing, and is the document in a safe place?

- With regard to a key employee, is there a replacement ready? Would the company be at risk if he or she was no longer with the company?

- If yours is a "family business," is the successor truly the most qualified person to take over?

CHAPTER 9

Develop Your People— It's Your Responsibility As Their Leader

ONE OF THE most important things you can do for your employees is to create an environment where they can reach their full potential.

Different people require different types of development. For example, putting all of your sales people in a single room to get identical sales training might not be the best use of your training dollars since not everyone has the same training needs. Before you can determine the best developmental program for an employee, you need to assess his or her unique strengths and weaknesses. Then you can find the most appropriate way to approach those unique needs so as to maximize the strengths and overcome the weaknesses. Mary might be so aggressive on cold calls that she needs some sensitivity training while Joe could be great at relationship building but is not comfortable with cold calling. Those who can successfully develop new business are much different from those who are adept at servicing customers. As such, they should be trained differently.

If you do a truly good job of developing employees to their full potential, you can expect some of them to leave the company. Losing a good employee is often unavoidable; that is, if you've developed an employee properly, and the employee outgrows the company, then him or her leaving you is inevitable. When that occurs, you should congratulate yourself for a job well done since you can look in the mirror and tell yourself that you did what was best for that individual. The employee leaves on good terms, moves to a greater career opportunity, and appreciates what you've done to make that advancement possible. It's tough to say goodbye, but it's the right thing to do.

If, on the other hand, a key employee leaves because you've failed to see or develop the potential that lies within, then shame on you. It's generally too late to make a counter-offer to someone who resigns but whom you really wish you could have retained. *Develop employees, and take care of them; don't take them for granted!*

Employee development is an ongoing process, not a one-time event. An ideal way to introduce employee development as a regular activity is to integrate it with performance appraisals. The employee and supervisor meet twice each year for the employee's performance appraisal, and together they identify areas where the employee needs to grow, either because of substandard performance or to prepare the employee for future advancement. Once the employee's developmental needs have been mutually agreed upon, a plan is prepared that will assist the employee in satisfying those needs. Not only is this procedure effective, but it also gives the employee the feeling that the company truly cares about his or her continued development, as evidenced by the company's willingness to provide the necessary help.

Example

The owner of a large manufacturing company took employee development so seriously that he created his own training facility and budgeted an amount equal to about two weeks' pay for each employee in the organization. The budget was established at the beginning of each fiscal year and was not reduced, even in years when the company's financial performance was adversely affected. Employee training and development were never to be short-changed.

Employees were very aware of this deeply-rooted value, and they truly appreciated that the company cared about their well-being. Likewise, the company realized it would lose certain employees who would, after extensive training and development at the company's expense, move on to other career opportunities outside of the company. Yet the company believed it had an ethical and moral obligation to help each employee reach his or her full potential.

The company integrated the training and development effort with performance appraisals in which individual needs were identified. During those same performance appraisal sessions, each employee and supervisor agreed upon specific quantitative standards of performance for the employee, as well as a reward system. Tying all of this together with training and development plans made it logical and easy for the employee to understand.

Check Your Shoes...

Before you move on to the next chapter, check the bottoms of your shoes to see whether you've avoided the entremanure:

- Are you proactively helping to develop your people, even if it means they might outgrow your company and go elsewhere?

- If an outsider asked your employees whether they feel like they are being "developed" for future advancement, would they answer "yes" or "no"?

- Do you work closely with employees to identify areas for development and then provide them with help in those areas (seminars, college courses, training, mentoring, and so on), at company expense?

- Are your employees fairly compensated? How do you know?

CHAPTER 10

Make the Tough Personnel Decisions— Now, Not Later

THE MOST DIFFICULT and gut-wrenching decisions to make are normally those that are personnel-related. No matter how much care is taken to put the right people in place, there will still be occasions when there is no choice but to remove or demote an employee. This is especially difficult in family businesses where relatives are often still on the job in spite of unacceptable performance.

Deal with it, and move on! The longer you tolerate a personnel problem, the harder it will be to handle it. Too often we hear of employees who have been terminated but truly had no idea they were in trouble! This is the result of weak leadership that repeatedly lacks the intestinal fortitude to tell an employee that a performance problem exists. It sometimes requires a single, monumental event to compel the owner finally to take action.

As stated in an earlier chapter, it's unfair to other employees if you don't hold all people to the same high standards of performance. If you find that good employees are leaving you but mediocre or substandard performers are hanging around, then you have a real problem.

If your organization is one that rewards people for longevity rather than performance, it's only a matter of time before you will pay the price. Many school systems are now suffering the consequences of rewarding people for tenure rather than for their abilities as teachers; as a result, they have faculties with far too many long-term employees who have outlived their effectiveness as teachers. Paying teachers based on performance rather than years of service would enable good teachers to earn significantly more income and make it worthwhile for them to remain in the profession that needs them so much. The private enterprise system is no different.

If your organization has effectively utilized job descriptions, measurable standards, and performance appraisals conducted twice each year, those steps can significantly simplify the process of weeding out substandard performers. If an employee clearly understands that there are specific, measurable standards that must be met, it will come as no surprise when a performance appraisal indicates a problem based on a failure to meet those standards.

Unfortunately, we often see employees continue to perform poorly but still receive pay increases. If an employee's performance falls short of the established standards, then no pay increase should be given. Instead, a plan should be created to raise the performance level. If that same employee's performance falls short again, it's time for termination. It's interesting to note that once employees understand they will be held accountable many of the substandard performers *weed themselves out* before having to be terminated. They know the system, and they realize there will be no more pay raises until they earn them, so they decide it's time to move on.

Although the process described above will dramatically reduce the number of performance-related terminations, there will still be occasions when it's necessary to separate an employee from the company. These are usually very difficult encounters for both parties. In spite of the emotion that surrounds these events, the dignity of the employee must always be considered. Remember that you, or someone in your company, was responsible for hiring the person in question. That error in judgment is partially to blame for the termination that now must take place. After laying out the documented, quantitative evidence of substandard performance, as well as the efforts that the company has made to assist the employee in meeting the standards, the conclusion becomes very logical and obvious to the employee. It's then a matter of trying to help the employee decide what career or company might be a good alternative for him or her to pursue. Although you may not be able to provide a good recommendation to that person's next employer, you can certainly offer guidance to the employee.

Example

A third-generation, family-owned manufacturing company had grown to $20 million in sales by providing precision-machined metal products to the aerospace industry.

Unlike many family-owned businesses, this particular family had enough foresight to hire a family business consultant to help it separate family issues from business issues. As a result, even though there were seventeen family members active in the business, they all agreed that only one of them was in charge of the day-to-day activities, and they followed his leadership as if they were not relatives.

The family's prior generation had hired a strong vice president of manufacturing when the company had reached $3 million in sales. He was well-liked by everyone, and some of the third-generation family members actually worked for him while they were learning the business.

When company sales passed $15 million, it became more and more obvious to the new generation of managers that the vice president of manufacturing just didn't have the capability of performing his duties in such a large production facility. There were actually engineers and other manufacturing personnel in the company who were more familiar with the latest technology and equipment. Yet everyone in the organization truly liked the vice president, which made it even more difficult to face up to the decision that needed to be made.

After the repeated advice of the company's outside board, the family member in charge finally met with the vice president to discuss the ever-increasing technical requirements of his job. When asked if he still felt comfortable with his position, the vice president said, "I've been uncomfortable for the past three years, but I've been afraid to say anything because I thought you'd ask me to retire early." After being assured that the company still had a place for him in a job he could handle, at a lower level in the organization, he breathed a sigh of relief and immediately accepted the alternative.

He understood that his new position would require that he receive no pay increases for at least three years, and he thought that was more than fair.

Because of the way the situation was handled, he was not only relieved but happy. His positive attitude regarding the ordeal quickly became apparent to everyone in the organization who knew, deep down, that he needed to step aside. The event that had been dreaded for so long had now made a positive impact on employee morale while enabling the company to bring in a highly qualified vice president of manufacturing who could lead future growth.

Not every personnel-related change results in a win-win situation like the one described above. Regardless of the outcome, though, making the necessary personnel decisions in a timely manner will increase your company's probability of success.

Check Your Shoes...

Before you move on to the next chapter, check the bottoms of your shoes to see whether you've avoided the entremanure:

- Do you have any poor-performing employees, including relatives, who need to be dealt with? Is this situation causing a morale problem in the company?

- Is it fair to you, the company, and the other employees, to allow poor performance to go un-addressed?

- Do you have a strong performer whose personal attitude can no longer be tolerated, in spite of his or her productivity or expertise? Are any employees "holding you hostage" because of their perceived importance in the company, even though their attitudes are not acceptable?

- If your organization is a "family company," have you effectively separated company business issues from family issues?

CHAPTER 11

Don't Give Stock to Employees—You're Likely to Regret It Later

MANY ENTREPRENEURS REWARD their employees with shares of stock, particularly in the early years. It's often used as a substitute for a cash bonus during a time when cash is limited. Although it seems like a good idea at the time, it usually isn't.

As your company grows, you typically find that the people who were "key" to your organization in the early years are not the ones who will be leaders in the future. Using the example from the previous chapter, the vice president of manufacturing in a company with $3 million in sales was not capable of handling the job when the company's volume reached $15 million. Consider what may have happened if the owner of the company had awarded shares of stock to the vice president of manufacturing when the company had sales of $3 million. Then, when a more qualified person became the new vice president of manufacturing, it would have created a situation in which a long-time employee who is perhaps two levels down in the organization actually owns 10 percent of the company's stock.

Awarding stock shares can also be an obstacle if you ever have to terminate an employee or if an employee dies and leaves the stock to a spouse or children. Or the new vice president of manufacturing might find it difficult to accept that someone lower in the organization is a shareholder; he or she might want the same share or more. In addition, a potential buyer might be reluctant to make an offer if it means dealing with too many shareholders.

If the purpose of rewarding stock is to provide an employee with an incentive to grow the company, then there are other methods that can accomplish the same thing without surrendering stock. Stock appreciation rights are becoming increasingly popular and provide a method of sharing a portion of the growth in the company's value.

For example, let's assume a company is deemed to have a value of $1 million on the day the new vice president of manufacturing comes on board and that the owner agrees to share 10 percent of future growth with the new vice president, vested at the rate of 20 percent per year over five years. Let's also assume that ten years later the company is sold for $10 million. Then, the vice president would be entitled to $900,000 (10 percent of the $9 million in growth during that time). That would be paid as ordinary income to the vice president, not as stock. If the vice president decides to leave before the company is sold, the amount due would be based on the value of the company at the time when the vice president departs. The formula for this calculation, as well as the timetable in which the payment is dispersed, would be decided upfront through a legal agreement.

Example

A sporting goods retailer hired a bright young college student to work part-time at his store located in a shopping mall near the main campus. When the student graduated two years later, the owner hired him as manager of his new store in another mall on the opposite side of town.

Under his direction, the new store grew rapidly and soon outperformed the original store. As a reward for his efforts, the young man was granted 5 percent of the shares of the company.

Four years later, the owner discovered that merchandise was missing from the store managed by his minority shareholder. After a quiet investigation, the owner learned that the young man had sold the merchandise and used the money to pay gambling debts.

Although he fired the young man immediately, 5 percent of the company's stock was still in the hands of the terminated employee. Because of the company's growth during the previous four years, there was a major controversy regarding the dollar value of the terminated employee's stock. The situation was eventually resolved, but the owner paid far more than it was worth.

Check Your Shoes…

Before you move on to the next chapter, check the bottoms of your shoes to see whether you've avoided the entremanure:

- Are you the only shareholder/owner? If you have employees who are shareholders, will they still be making valuable contributions to your success when your company gets much larger, or will the company outgrow their capabilities?

- Do you have a legal agreement describing the precise steps required to purchase stock from a shareholder and providing a specific formula for how to value the stock?

- Within the past year, have you had an attorney review all of the conditions pertaining to the purchase of stock from other shareholders?

CHAPTER 12

If Possible, Avoid Having Family Members in the Business

IT WOULD BE great to provide example after example of businesses that have run smoothly and successfully with family members working side by side on a daily basis. Although it's certainly possible, the majority of "family businesses" are filled with challenges.

Even though your business might not be classified as a "family business" today, there's a good chance that at least one member of your family will eventually join your enterprise, probably before you retire and typically much sooner than that.

The family businesses that are able to overcome potential pitfalls are normally those that have separated business issues from family issues. It's best to involve a professional advisor who specializes in working with family businesses so that the line can be drawn between the business enterprise and family unit *before* a situation arises that can be a source of conflict—sort of a "prenuptial" agreement.

Most entrepreneurs who bring family members into the business feel very confident they'll be able to handle any potential conflicts that might arise. After all, "we're family!" But what if it *doesn't* work? Can you fire or demote your brother, sister, child, parent, spouse, or other relative? If you do find the strength to fire a family member (and many people just can't do it), what will happen to your relationships with other family members? Will you ever be accepted at the family reunion or barbecue?

If your brother is active in the business with you, and the two of you are lucky enough to get along well with one another, how will your spouse feel when your brother takes too much time off or isn't "pulling his weight" for some reason? Or, if you have a dispute with your brother, will your mother or father get dragged into it by being asked to take sides?

What if you bring your son or daughter into the business? Will other key employees feel threatened or see their career paths blocked? And how do you handle the situation if one of your children is interested in growing the business while another wants to sell it? What if one is active in the business and the other isn't—how do you "keep things even" between them?

These are only a few of the countless issues that can arise. It doesn't mean that you and your family are doomed; it simply means that you must separate the family issues from the business issues and be prepared for possible conflicts in areas that you cannot foresee at the outset. It requires consultation with an expert, as well as interaction with other entrepreneurs who have already been through this kind of situation. Many communities have informal discussion groups in which owners of family businesses can meet periodically to share their experiences.

If you do decide to bring a family member into your business, first have that person work for another company to gain some valuable experience. If he or she would still like to join your company after three to five years working for someone else, make the hiring decision in the same manner you would make it if the candidate were not related to you. Do you have a vacant position? Is he or she qualified? If so, adhere to the same screening and interviewing process as any other candidate. Structure a compensation plan that is fair—no more, no less. Be sure that he or she reports to someone in your organization who is not a family member and who will not be afraid to be critical or tough when necessary. Under no circumstance should you ever encourage a family member to circumvent the chain of command by coming to you with a problem that should be handled elsewhere in the organization.

The bottom line is this—if you really want one or more family members in the business, go to great lengths to lay out all the rules before you do it.

Example

George retired from a major university at age fifty-five, after teaching computer science classes for twenty-five years. During his time as a professor, George had been involved as a consultant with a major hotel chain, where he became an expert at gathering and analyzing government statistics to assist the chain in making decisions about the locations of new hotels.

After his retirement from the university, George developed some proprietary software that enabled him to conduct these same types of analyses in seconds rather than hours. He began to make the service available to a variety of national retailers who relied on his company to provide them with the data they needed to make decisions about potential new retail sites. George was the sole shareholder of his new company.

George had a son, Mark, and the two of them were very close. Mark had been a systems analyst at a large company in the same vicinity. When George's company reached the point where volume could justify the addition of a key employee, George invited Mark to join him. The two arrived at a financial arrangement that would allow Mark to purchase 20 percent of George's stock.

Initially, the two struggled regarding their roles in the organization. George was now in his early sixties and wanted to spend less time with the business. He did not believe, however, that Mark was ready to take over. By the third year, Mark began to resent the fact that his father was spending only two days each week at work yet would not allow Mark to take over officially. To make matters worse, Mark felt as though he was doing nearly all the work but still held only 20 percent of the stock. Soon, Mark's wife began to resent George for being unfair to Mark. Family relationships became strained.

One evening, after Mark and his wife realized the situation was actually taking its toll on their marriage, Mark knew he had to confront his father. They arranged to meet for dinner after work. When Mark told George about his frustration, George was both disappointed and hurt. When George tried to explain to Mark that he didn't think Mark was ready to run the company, Mark informed George that he would be leaving the organization to take another job. George's reaction went from disappointment to anger, and the two raised their voices with one another for the first time in their lives. When Mark's mother learned of the argument, she couldn't bear to see Mark and George at odds with one another, so she confided in a friend whose husband had three of the couple's children involved in the family landscaping business. Her friend strongly recommended a family business advisor who had been of immense help when her family had confronted a similar conflict a few years earlier.

Mark and George agreed to meet with the same family business advisor, who immediately forced them to deal with family issues separately from business operations. In addition, the family business advisor urged George and Mark to create an outside board of independent business advisors to help them with issues associated with day-to-day operations. The outside advisors would be in a much better position to evaluate objectively whether or not Mark was ready to take over.

Although the entire process took eleven months to resolve, the result was that George agreed to become chairman, Mark moved to vice president of operations, and they hired a fifty-eight-year-old professional manager from the outside to serve as president for three to five years, depending upon how long it took Mark to prepare for the position of president as determined by the outside board of advisors. During that same timeframe Mark gradually purchased more and more stock from George. Interestingly, when the outside board of advisors finally agreed that Mark was ready to take over, Mark decided he wanted to spend more time writing code than managing people, so the outside president remained.

Check Your Shoes...

Before you move on to the next chapter, check the bottoms of your shoes to see whether you've avoided the entremanure:

• Do you have any relatives in the business, or do you expect a relative to join you in the future? If so, is he or she *truly* qualified for the position? Would you hire "an outsider" who had identical qualifications? Would the outsider be paid at the same rate as your relative? Is your relative being held to the same performance standards as others, including hours worked?

• If you have a relative in the business, would others in your company agree with the answers you provided to the questions above?

CHAPTER 13

Always Be Fair, and Set a Good Example

FAIRNESS IS A relative term. What seems fair to one employee might not seem fair to another. These types of discrepancies can usually be avoided by establishing a formalized set of policies and procedures—not a thick booklet, but a concise and clearly presented set of guidelines by which employees govern themselves.

When a situation arises that can't easily be resolved using the formalized set of policies and procedures, take the time to gather the facts, step back and objectively evaluate those facts, and make a decision you would think is fair if you were on either side of the issue. If you're not sure, seek the advice of an objective third party whom you respect. When you finally make a ruling, do it decisively but diplomatically, and feel good about it. Keep in mind that some people are never satisfied, and not every situation will be a pleasant one. The important thing is to be fair.

Being fair also means you should be fair to yourself. If an employee's poor performance is affecting the business, not only do you have the right to take corrective action, but you may also have the *duty* to do so if you have other shareholders.

Setting a good example is not as easy as it may sound. If you're still the one who is running the business on a day-to-day basis, be on time for work. Never ask anyone to do something you're not willing to do yourself. Take the parking spot that's farthest from the building so your employees can park closer than you. Don't fly first class when you expect your employees to fly coach. Answer your own phone, get your own coffee, and don't hesitate to make a new pot of coffee when you take the last cup. It's the little things that make a difference!

Example

When Joyce started her own home-cleaning business, she literally did every job. Each time she hired another employee, she worked side-by-side with that person to demonstrate the correct way to do things. When the business had five employees, she was forced to spend less time cleaning so that she could do the scheduling, sales, bookkeeping, and billing. In spite of these additional tasks, Joyce also served as a fill-in employee anytime someone was absent. Her employees were incredibly loyal to her and truly appreciated the fact that no job was beneath her.

Joyce was proud of what she and her company had achieved, and she was anxious for her daughter, Rachel, to walk in her footsteps. After graduating from high school, Rachel joined the business with her mother. Like Joyce, Rachel was taught every job. There was, though, one subtle difference between mother and daughter that the employees soon detected. Because Joyce wanted the best for Rachel, she soon delegated the scheduling and bookkeeping to Rachel. When someone was absent from the cleaning crew, it wasn't Rachel who filled in—it was Joyce.

Before long, the employees started referring to Rachel as "Golden Child" whenever Joyce and Rachel weren't around. They lost some respect for Joyce, not because Joyce wasn't being fair to them but because she wasn't being fair to herself. Joyce had created a culture built on her sense of fair play and equality, yet she had made an exception in the case of her own daughter.

After two years, Rachel decided to go back to school for a degree in geology. Shortly thereafter, Joyce hired a part-time scheduler and bookkeeper, and she went back to her role as a fill-in during employee absences, as well as some selling whenever time allowed. "Golden Child" had moved on to other things, and the culture at Joyce's company was once again built on fairness and equality.

Check Your Shoes...

Before you move on to the next chapter, check the bottoms of your shoes to see whether you've avoided the entremanure:

- Do you ever ask employees to do anything you wouldn't be willing to do yourself?

- Do you park your vehicle closest to the building, or do you make a special effort so that your customers, visitors, and employees can park closer than you?

- Do you treat employees fairly and equally?

- If your employees were asked to describe you and your company to their friends, what do you think they would say?

Have a Plan, in Writing, and Keep It Up to Date

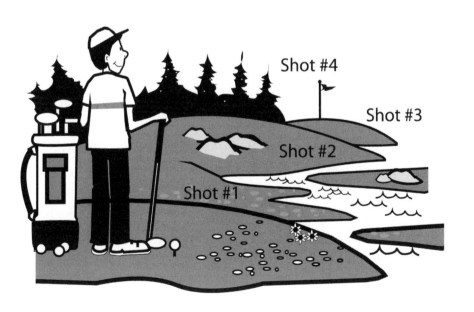

Shot #4

Shot #3

Shot #2

Shot #1

IT MAY SEEM strange that the subject of planning isn't addressed until chapter 14, since planning is so essential to the success of any enterprise. The reasoning is based on the experiences I've had in facilitating the planning process—that is, I have often been called in to assist a business owner and his or her executive team with planning, only to find that many of the people in the room had been promoted beyond their individual levels of competency. Therefore, before you engage your company in the planning process, you should first address the many personnel issues that have already been covered in earlier chapters. Having the right people on board to create and implement the plan is essential.

There's a saying: "If you don't know where you're going, any road will get you there." The importance of planning is often overlooked. Most people who go into business for themselves will tell you they were tired of working for someone else or didn't feel like they had any job security. Yet they're willing to risk everything they have without a formal plan of some type—that's even less secure than remaining with an employer who controls your destiny.

Have a plan! You need to think of planning in two categories. First, have a life plan for yourself and your family; that is, lay out a realistic vision of the life you'd like to have. Then, prepare a long-range plan for your company that will allow you to realize the dream you have for yourself and family.

In preparing your personal plan, involve your spouse, family, and any business partners you have in creating your vision. Entrepreneurs are generally pretty good at verbalizing what they want their lives to be like as it pertains to themselves and their families, but they often forget to speak openly with their business partners and employees to understand what they hope to achieve and by when. Discussing this topic upfront can prevent a lot of problems later. This is particularly important when there is an age gap between owners, often creating a situation where an older partner wants to sell the business in five years while a younger partner wants to hold on to it.

The preparation of a written plan for a business is a much more methodical process than simply thinking about what you want to do. There are countless books and seminars devoted to planning, but the vast majority take the same approach. Frankly, it doesn't matter which book you read or which seminar you take; the important thing is that you *follow the process!*

There seems to be some type of mystique about "planning." People get too concerned about semantics, like "mission" versus "vision," "problems" versus "threats," "strategies" versus "tactics," "core competency" versus "sustainable competitive advantage," "goals" versus "objectives," and so on. Planning can be presented in a very academic fashion by a university professor or in a very simple and pragmatic way by someone else. The fact is, *it's not rocket science!* Planning is a very logical thought process that systematically leads you to some conclusions as to how you should proceed. Don't be intimidated by it!

Accept the fact that planning is a process, not a project. Done correctly, planning goes on at all times, and your plan is likely to get modified every time a major fact changes. It's a lot like playing golf, standing on the tee, ready to launch your drive. The process usually begins when you determine where the hole (goal) is and realize there are a number of ways to get there. Before you can choose the most appropriate route, you have to consider the environment—Is it raining? Is the wind blowing? If so, in what direction? Am I ahead of the competition and should therefore play conservatively, or am I behind and need to take some chances?

Once you've considered the environment, you will likely look at the hole and work backwards shot-by-shot in your mind to determine each step you plan to take. Now you have a plan! But after your drive, you find yourself behind a tree, which is not what you had planned. The goal might still be the same (shoot par on the hole), but the other steps in the plan may have to be altered. In fact, it might be necessary to admit you'll have to plan for an extra shot rather than a par, based on the position you're in after your tee shot.

Planning is no different than the golfing example. If you try to bull your way forward without keeping your head up, you won't notice that some of the environmental factors around you have changed, thereby requiring you to modify your plan a bit.

Also, make the plan as simple and understandable as possible. It need not be lengthy. There are some truly excellent plans that are only a page or two and, because of their simplicity, can be thoroughly understood by everyone in an organization.

Once the plan is prepared, set quantifiable, realistic objectives to be met along the way so you can be absolutely certain you are on target. Typical quantifiable measures include sales, gross profit, net profit, market share, market rank, productivity per employee, return on investment, number of new customers, employee retention rate, and so on.

Example

This example is actually two in one, and it's presented here to demonstrate the value of a simple but well-documented plan. A group of potential investors had invited two well-established companies to make presentations to them so the investors could evaluate both potential expansion opportunities.

The first company was a manufacturer of automotive engine cooling parts. Representatives from the company entered the room with a stack of three-ring binders, which they proceeded to distribute to those in the room. They then began a ninety-minute slide presentation that was very professionally done and extremely well-documented. After about twenty minutes, some of the investors started to flip to the back of the book, where the financial projections were included, while a few others seemed to be daydreaming. Nonetheless, the plan was well done, and the company presented a very attractive investment opportunity.

After a short break, representatives from the second company entered the room. They, too, were in the automotive parts business but were manufacturers of rubber engine components. Their presentation consisted of eleven slides, copies of which were distributed at the outset. They also had three-ring binders, but the binders were distributed after their twenty-minute presentation and contained all the necessary back-up details for those who wished to review those materials. During the twenty minutes, all investors were paying attention, and there were questions and answers for a period of about twenty-five minutes after the presentation.

Although both companies actually received funding as a result of their presentations, it was very interesting to see how the audience reacted to the two different approaches. Perhaps the most important thing to note from this example is that if these two companies had to rely strictly on their written plans to attract investors, it is much more likely that the second company would have been successful since it "presented its case" very quickly and simply rather than requiring investors to read through volumes of information.

Although plans are not always written to seek funding or approval by the capital budgeting committee of a corporation, it's often said that the typical reader will devote between 1 ½ and 2 ½ minutes to reading a plan. The lesson in this story is to make sure your plan has a brief but comprehensive executive summary that will compel the reader to take a closer look. Remember that the document should stand on its own since in many cases you don't get the opportunity to present it in person.

Check Your Shoes…

Before you move on to the next chapter, check the bottoms of your shoes to see whether you've avoided the entremanure:

- Do you have a plan for your company? Is it in writing? Is it up to date?

- Do you have a plan for your life? Is it in writing? Is it up to date?

- Is there consistency between the plan you have for your company and the plan you have for your life? Do your life plan and business plan have specific, quantifiable goals and timeframes in which they are to be achieved?

- Have you asked a trusted, objective advisor to read your life plan and business plan and to provide you with a critique?

CHAPTER 15

Develop a Formalized Organization Structure, with Written Job Descriptions

STRUCTURE *COMES AFTER* strategy, but they're often reversed. Determine what the organization will look like only *after* the plan is prepared. The reason is simple—unless you know where you're going, you can't determine the organization you'll need to get there.

It's similar to a military general who first assesses the enemy, formulates a plan of attack, and then selects the formation and personnel who will be most effective in carrying out the plan. For a company, it's best to consider the plan first, then determine the best structure to achieve the plan and draw the "boxes." Finally, it's time to define the qualities of the ideal candidate for each box (without using the names of any candidates at this point).

Only after formulating the profile of the ideal candidate should you look at your current group of employees to determine whether anyone "fits." By the time you complete the process, you'll probably find that a few current employees actually do fit, a few are close and could possibly be developed through proper training, and there will probably be a few positions that will require you to go outside your organization to find qualified candidates. Whatever you do, don't try to make someone "fit" into a spot for which he or she isn't qualified. It's tempting to use all of your current employees to fill the new boxes, but that's a little bit like rearranging the chairs on the deck of the Titanic!

Each position in your organization should have a written job description. There are many "how to" books available to assist you in putting together job descriptions, or you might prefer to have a human resources consultant help you with this task. Once the format is established, each job description can be prepared in a consistent manner.

Job descriptions should be kept up to date, since the structure will change as the strategy changes. To make sure job descriptions stay current, formally assign that duty to someone in your organization.

Example

A successful marketing research company decided that it had the telephone dialing equipment and capacity to enter a new market—collecting bad debts from consumers.

The owner did extensive research regarding the "collections" business and became familiar with all the regulations that governed the industry. He hired a professional trainer to educate his marketing research employees so they could begin to make "collection" calls during evenings and on weekends while adhering to the industry's strict legal regulations.

The owner had previously established job descriptions for his marketing research staff, but he failed to write job descriptions for those who were making collection calls, even though these were the same employees. He initially selected three women in their fifties to begin making collection calls since they were more mature and less likely to be rude and violate the strict laws governing telephone collections.

After three weeks, one of the telephone collectors used unacceptable language in dealing with someone who had become irate when she called. The company fired her on the spot, after which she filed suit against the employer for requiring her to perform duties not in her job description and suggesting that she and the other two ladies were put in that situation because of their age. The owner settled with the employee out of court and quickly sought the assistance of an outside consultant to create a new job description and to review all of the other job descriptions through-out the company.

Check Your Shoes...

Before you move on to the next chapter, check the bottoms of your shoes to see whether you've avoided the entremanure:

- Do you have a job description for every position in your organization, including your own?

- Do you have an employee handbook that includes specific policies and procedures?

- Do you have a compensation system that ranks positions, with appropriate pay ranges?

CHAPTER 16

Manage Employee Performance Using Established Standards and Expectations

CHAPTER 4, THE most important chapter in this book, stressed how important it is that an organization is staffed with the best people available. No matter how strong an employee might be, there is still a need to establish standards of performance and be sure those standards are clearly communicated. Otherwise, even the best employee can sometimes fall short yet never realize there was a shortcoming.

The vast majority of employee terminations can easily be handled if the employee and supervisor agree, upfront, on *specifically* what the expected outcome is to be. It is likely to require some discussion before both parties actually agree on what's expected, and it often requires the supervisor to offer some type of help in the form of training, education, or tools if the expected outcome is to be achieved. It is also extremely important that the employee knows exactly what reward awaits him or her if the outcome is achieved; conversely, the consequences of "falling short" must also be clearly communicated. To reinforce the process, performance should be monitored along the way to make sure the employee is progressing according to schedule, and to determine whether there is anything more the employee needs in order to meet the expected outcome.

The reward for meeting or exceeding the agreed-upon outcome should be commensurate with the task. Ideally, every incentive compensation system should be based on activities that are *within the control of the employee* so as not to provide an employee with a "windfall" reward he or she doesn't deserve and not to penalize an employee by denying a reward that *is* deserved.

Above all, avoid discretionary bonuses! They become viewed as entitlements by employees, and, once you start the practice of playing "Santa Claus" by distributing bonuses on a discretionary basis, it's extremely difficult to stop the practice. So, don't start! Instead, take the time to design a formula for each employee that directly correlates his or her incentive compensation to some quantitative measure of performance. If the calculation shows no bonus is due, then none should be paid. If, on the other hand, performance has exceeded expectations by a wide margin, don't hesitate to pay the amount due, no matter how much it is. (Note: It's essential that you work through all possible scenarios when creating an incentive compensation formula so you don't find yourself in a situation unfair to your employee or yourself. Seek outside help if you need it.)

Financial incentives can be established so that they are paid on a deferred basis, annually, quarterly, monthly, daily, or hourly. Generally, the further down an employee is on the organization chart, the more frequently a financial incentive should be paid.

Example

John joined a small manufacturing company as production manager. At the end of his first year on the job, plant production was 20 percent ahead of the prior year, and product quality had not deteriorated. John was pleased with his accomplishments and looked forward to meeting the owner of the company, who would be conducting John's performance appraisal. Unfortunately, the meeting did not go as John had anticipated since the owner had expected a 26 percent increase in production, which was the level of volume necessary for the company to meet demand for its products and to maintain its share of the rapidly growing market. There were excessive back orders, and inventories were at an all-time low.

John received no bonus due to the shortfall, but the situation could have been avoided if the performance standards had been made clear—for example, 26 percent increase in production, no drop in quality level, back orders below two weeks, and a six to eight week supply of inventories. The failure of the owner to present John with his goals at the beginning of the year actually made things unpleasant for both of them. The proper procedure would have been for John and the owner to sit down at the outset of the year, jointly review the industry forecast and company budget, and together arrive at the production goal for the year, as well as the goals for quality, back orders, and inventory levels. Once they had both agreed, then it would have been John's responsibility to determine how to achieve the goals and the owner's responsibility to give John the tools necessary to accomplish them.

Check Your Shoes…

Before you move on to the next chapter, check the bottoms of your shoes to see whether you've avoided the entremanure:

- Do you have performance standards for all job descriptions that are *quantitative and measurable*?

- Do your employees know exactly what is expected of them?

- Do you hold employees accountable for their performance versus the established standards?

- Do your employees think you believe performance appraisals are important?

- Do you have an established process for conducting employee performance appraisals twice per year, including a comparison of actual performance versus expectations as defined in the quantitative standards for the position?

- Do you have a compensation system that includes incentives linked to measurable standards?

CHAPTER 17

Leverage the Wisdom of Others by Setting up an Outside Board: It's by Far the Best Way to Avoid the Entremanure!

YOUR COMPANY IS never too small to seek the advice of qualified, *objective* outsiders. These are people who have already walked through the entrepreneurial pasture and have probably gotten their shoes dirty a few times. Learn from them; they'll be anxious to help! Even if you're a "one-person show," find yourself a mentor who isn't enamored with your business, and meet periodically on an informal basis to discuss the issues that confront you.

Better yet, put together a more formal group with a specific meeting schedule, typically quarterly. Meetings can be a few hours or a full day. Have an agenda for each meeting, and ask the members to help you identify topics they believe are "key issues" for you.

For companies with fewer than two hundred employees, a group of three unbiased outsiders is usually adequate. They should be from different disciplines, such as finance, marketing, or operations. They should also be experts in their fields. They'll bring you the kind of talent you probably can't afford on a day-to-day basis. Their focus should be primarily on the more strategic issues facing you, but you can expect them to get involved in other areas as well. By no means do you want them to get into the minute details of your operation, but they can certainly provide you with guidance in those areas.

Some companies prefer boards of directors whereas others choose boards of advisors. There is a legal difference, so you should consult your attorney before you decide how you want to structure your board. Although it's certainly acceptable to have an attorney, accountant, and so forth on your board, do *not* have *your* attorney, accountant, or other paid advisors join your board since you're already paying them for their advice and because there's always a chance they might not be as objective as those who have nothing to gain or lose by providing you advice. You absolutely *must* have independent thinkers!

Before deciding what types of people you need, take a candid look at your organization to determine its greatest weaknesses. Then identify potential outside board candidates who could help you overcome those weaknesses.

When you form your board, be sure to establish term limits from the very start, and stagger them so that only one member leaves and is replaced at a time. Typical term limits are one, two, or three years. They provide you and the member with the opportunity to sever the relationship or, if appropriate, extend the engagement for another term, usually one additional year at a time. In the majority of cases, either the business owner or board member will conclude it's time to end the engagement after four or five years since by then the board member will have imparted the majority of his or her expertise. In addition, after a few years you are likely to find that your needs have changed—for example, you may have been weak in marketing when you formed your board, but three years later you may have a strong full-time marketing person join your company and, therefore, no longer need that type of expertise from your board.

You should also give each board member a letter of indemnification so that he or she is personally indemnified by you in the event that the board is named in a legal proceeding. An alternative is "Directors and Officers Insurance," but it is an expense that can often be avoided by offering a simple letter of indemnification. It is also common practice to ask each board member to sign a confidentiality agreement since proprietary information will be disclosed by the company.

Although many board members do not expect to be paid, it is a good idea to offer them compensation commensurate with their experience levels. Some might prefer that you donate the money to a charity in their name. Others will serve simply because they enjoy it. The bottom line is this—if the first question a member asks is how much he or she will be compensated, then you've made the wrong choice!

Board members can come from a variety of sources. If you don't know any potential candidates, ask your attorney or accountant to give you some names. If they can't supply you with some good candidates, then you should probably find another attorney or accountant.

When you meet to "interview" the potential board candidate for the first time, be sure to have a booklet put together that describes your company, in much the same way you would want to familiarize a new employee with your operation—company history, organization chart, a description of what you do, your products/services, the markets/customers you serve, some basic financial numbers (but nothing proprietary during the interview), and your expectations from each board member.

After you've found your first board member, it's often a good idea for the two of you to find the next member *together* since this will make it less likely that there could be a personality conflict between members.

These are only a few of the procedures to follow when you put together an outside board. There are countless books on the topic, including ones on the legal ramifications of various board structures.

In this final chapter, it seems redundant to follow the same format ("Example" and "Check Your Shoes") as in the previous sixteen chapters since, frankly, *I can't think of an example of an unsuccessful company that has an independent outside board.* As for "Check Your Shoes," you either have an outside board, or you don't; it's that simple! Therefore, the most important thing to remember is this—*if you do not have an outside board, get one... NOW!*

Author Bill Matthews, Ph.D.

ABOUT THE AUTHOR

AFTER SPENDING A few years as a teacher and coach, Bill Matthews entered the business world, where he gained a wide range of experience. He served as a high-level executive and corporate officer for a *Fortune* 500 company, president of a privately-held regional financial services business that was purchased by a publicly-traded corporation, and also spent a few years in a small family-owned enterprise. With that broad base of managerial exposure, he was invited by Clay Mathile, former owner of The Iams Company, to help create and launch Aileron (www.aileron.net). Based in Dayton, Ohio, Aileron is a not-for-profit entity whose focus is the implementation of professional management systems in privately-owned businesses. During his years with Aileron, Bill has worked with the leaders of hundreds of businesses to assist them with professional management, strategic planning, and the establishment of outside boards.

If you have questions or comments regarding this book, you can reach Bill at: bill.matthews@aileron.net.

INDEX

training, 46, 64–66, 94, 98
transferring a business, 20

under-capitalization, 26
unexpected death, 21

vision, 15, 22–23, 53–55

will, 61